GW00481279

Littlehampton

in old picture postcards

by
Tony Wales

European Library – Zaltbommel/Netherlands

By the same author:
We Wunt be Druv, 1976.
A Sussex Garland, 1979.
The West Sussex Village Book, 1984.
Horsham in old picture postcards, volume 1, 1987; volume 2, 1992.
An Album of Old Horsham, 1989.
Sussex Customs, Curiosities and Country Lore, 1990.
Horsham Guides, 1985, 1987, 1990.
Sussex Ghosts and Legends, 1992.

GB   ISBN 90 288 5559 9 / CIP

INTRODUCTION

First of all my credentials and an admission. I was not born in Littlehampton and have never lived there permanently. However, I spent many of my childhood days there during the summer months, staying with my grandparents, who lived in the town in the 1920s and '30s.

My own memories are of a small, friendly town, dominated by the river and its fascinating industries. From my grandparents' house I could reach the town via a series of Twittens (Sussex name for narrow alleyways), always ending up in Pier Road, with its engrossing mixture of watery sights and smells. Over it all was the ever present sound of the steam-powered saw in John Eede Butt's timber yard.

Often accompanied by my grandparents' dog, I spent many happy, sunshiny days among the lobster pots and fishing boats, oblivious to everything else including regular meal times.

The windmill was also part of my childhood and I can recall the shock when my grandfather told me that it was to be taken down. I appreciated Mr. Butlin's amusements that appeared in its place, but I would have preferred to have had both.

Littlehampton has much to interest historians. At least from Norman times the Arun has been an important river route, with Arundel as the main port, once capable of dealing with quite large boats. Even as late as the 1890s the riverside area of the town was considered quite separate to the residential part, long known simply as Beach. Surprisingly in 1965 Nikolaus Pevsner could still describe the two areas of the town as 'a mixture of old Hastings and Bournemouth'. Imperceptibly the place gained a reputation as a holiday resort, with several well-known literary and artistic figures giving it their seal of approval.

In 1834 'The Gentleman's Magazine' had this to say about the town: *Littlehampton has acquired many warm friends, who consider it unrivalled by any watering-places on the southern coast for the convenience of bathing, and the salubrity and free circulation of fine air. The principal houses stand on a terrace placed about 200 yards from the sea, a distance which is increased to half a mile at low water... The mildness of the climate is shown by the myrtles which grow in the open air against the houses.*

But not all writers were so kind. Early in the present century another commentator had this to say:

It is a good place for children and girls in their teens, a bad one for men and women. The 'flies' (carriages) are awful. There is nothing to do, and no one to do it with; cooking and amusements do not exist.

The most significant part of the passage is that which refers to children. That Littlehampton was and still is a very happy place for children, all are agreed.

The growth of the town is shown by the population figures. In 1801 it was a mere 584, rising to 2,270 by 1841, and 5,950 in 1901. By the time the railways came to the town in the mid-nineteenth century, the claims of Littlehampton to be a pleasant coastal holiday resort, with particular charms for children, had become widely accepted.

Trade was also increasing, with shipbuilding, fishing and imports through the harbour, with coal, timber and other items arriving regularly.

History did not stop in the nineteenth century; for instance there was the particular magic of the annual Fair Day (26th May) which took place in Surrey Street and the area known as the Fisherman's Quay. This was reputed to be one of the oldest chartered fairs in the country, with the fair people and their families arriving in the town just before six o'clock on the previous evening. Apart from one or two definite sites, each group had to grab whatever place they could as the clock struck six. Members of each would dash through the site, carrying a pole to thrust into the ground to claim their favourite spot. The Roundabout always had a fixed site, right at the water's edge, so that the accompanying row of swings could appear to hang over the water at high tide. 1933 was the last year the Fair was allowed into Surrey Street, the following year it was moved to Linden Park, where it was allowed to stay longer than one day – but all the glamour had gone!

'Rough Music' was invoked when someone had offended the local community and had to be punished. The custom of men and boys assembling outside the culprit's house after dark, was recorded in 1859 when Mr. Sutton, a local watchmaker, was serenaded with pots and pans, for the imagined ill-treatment of his wife.

The nineteenth century poor were not ignored and in the 1880s the Terminus Hotel was used to provide a soup kitchen during several hard winters, with 'nourishing soup' being dispensed at one penny a quart, plus another penny for a quartern loaf.

In slightly more modern times much attention was given in Littlehampton Guide Books to the hours of sunshine recorded each summer, and it was then that the town really became 'The Children's Paradise'. I am not alone in recalling the joys of the Arcade as a child, or the satisfaction afforded by the fine sands, varied with shows by pierrots and Punch and Judy. In the 1980s a lady told me that her particular childhood memory was in dashing to the Arcade shortly after arrival, to the Bazaar on the right-hand corner, where it was possible to purchase a wooden canoe complete with Indian with a feather head-dress, all for sixpence ($2\frac{1}{2}$ p).

Came the time in the early 1930s when Billy Butlin's Amusements appeared on the sea front. Most of the Mums were horrified and one is noted as saying that it was 'The end of the world'. But of course the children loved the 'Bumper Cars' and the big 'Thriller', and whatever one thought of the Amusement Park from an architectural viewpoint, this obviously added the final ingredient to a seaside town just made for children's tastes.

Littlehampton has been well served with local photographers. The best known was probably John White, who started in business in the town in 1874 with, it was said, money gained as a reward for catching a smuggler – another sidelight on Littlehampton's history. His business continued through three generations until 1968. Then there was Alfred King, who started on his own in 1880, taking over an existing business. He retired in 1910. The third locally famous name was that of Frank Spry who came to Littlehampton in 1904, working for John White. In 1907 he opened on his own, and his shop and studio remained in Surrey Street until the Second World War. This is a good place to mention a modern photographer and local historian, who did so much to record the annals of the town in relatively recent times. He was Mr. H.J.F. 'Jack' Thompson, who died in 1985, having assembled a huge collection of Littlehampton pictures gathered from many sources, including of course his own photographs. He also wrote a number of pictorial books, leaving us details of many facets of the town through its photographic history. He moved to Littlehampton as a young boy with his parents and took up photography after the Second World War, becoming a founder member of Littlehampton and District Camera Club. Almost without intending to, he became the town's leading local historian and was always ready to share his encyclopedic knowledge with others, as I can well testify.

In my own modest selection of old photographs I have not attempted to provide a comprehensive, pictorial view of the town, but instead have concentrated on some of the more unusual pictures, which have, in the main, not appeared in print elsewhere. There are already a number of excellent books which include many interesting photographs of some of the more obvious subjects, so if these are missing from this collection, it is only because I felt it better to concentrate on other views which had not already been seen.

Time often plays strange tricks with memory, so if there are any corrections or additions which readers can offer, I will be happy to receive them.

Acknowledgements

I am very grateful to the following who have contributed postcards, photographs or memories, during the time I have been compiling this book – and in some cases some time before I even anticipated working on such a project: Mr. J. Cannon, Mrs. E. Corfield, Mr. C.W. Cramp, Mrs. S. D'Arcy-Fox, Dr. I. Friel and the staff of Littlehampton Museum, Lens of Sutton, Mrs. L. Poston, Mr. R. Richardson, Miss A. Robinson, Mrs. A.C.M. Taylor, Mr. G. Thompson and the late Mr. H.J.F. Thompson.

Bibliography

Elleray, D.Robert: Littlehampton: A Pictorial History, 1991.

Gill, W.H: Songs of the British Folk, ND.

Hannah, Ian.C: The Sussex Coast, 1912.

Hoare, John: Sussex Railway Architecture, 1979.

Horsfield, Thomas Walker: The History, Antiquities and Topography of the County of Sussex, 1835.

Jones, Iris and Stanford, Daphne: Littlehampton in Old Photographs, 1990.

Kelly's Directory of Sussex, 1903.

Littlehampton Guides, various years.

Marshall, C.F.Dendy: A History of the Southern Railway, 1936.

Richards, Sam: The English Folksinger, 1979.

Thompson, H.J.F: Littlehampton Long Ago, 1974.
    Littlehampton Through the Wars, 1978.
    The Swing Bridge Story, 1979.
    The Picturemakers, 1981.

Turner, J.T.Howard: The London, Brighton and South Coast Railway. 1, 2, 3, 1977, 1978, 1979.

Wymer, Norman: Companion into Sussex, 1950.

The Sussex County Magazine.

The West Sussex Gazette.

1. *Littlehampton sea front.* An old print of c1860 (reproduced on a postcard) showing the foreshore and South Terrace. The masts of several sailing ships can be seen in the harbour, also the lighthouse and mill. The promenade was not built until 1867, so at this time the famous 'Green' ran into the sands. Several folk are enjoying themselves and there is even a horse-drawn gig moving eastwards at what appears to be a spanking pace. It was possible to take a horse and carriage along the sands as far as Worthing at low tide, and the Green must have been a popular place with horseriders at this period.

Parade and Beach, Littlehampton

2. *The Promenade*. A typical sea-front view c1911, with the ladies in their voluminous dresses much in evidence. The handwritten message on the back of the card (posted to Croydon in July 1911) says it all: 'Weather glorious. Had a happy time on the sands this morning. She did enjoy herself – now sleeping.' On the beach side of the prom, at that time devoid of kiosks or any other buildings, is a line of portable bathing tents, which had replaced the earlier wheeled bathing huts. One lady speaking to me of these tents, said that they were 'all the rage' when they first appeared. The children, just a little less over-dressed than the adults (although still well covered by modern standards), are enjoying one of the sunny days in the halcyon period before the First World War.

3. *The beach.* A lively scene on Littlehampton's sands, which were often referred to as 'The Children's Paradise'. The card is undated, but it must be early in this century, possibly just into the 1920s. Of particular interest is the pedlar, with his tray of Rowntree's chocolate bars. There were many additional attractions arranged with children in mind; such as sand castle competitions, judged by an Uncle Dan or Uncle Terry. The winners chose a children's annual as a prize (out of date, but still acceptable). Some of the sand castles were really well done, embellished with shells and pieces of chalk, or even bought items such as paper flags. Later in this period there was the opportunity to watch out for 'Mr. Lobby Ludd', who represented a national newspaper. If you spotted him and used the correct challenge, you were rewarded with a prize. By the 1930s roving cameramen were a common sight in the seafront area, snapping away at holidaymakers and presenting them with a piece of paper which invited the holder to claim a photo later the same day – for a small fee of course.

LITTLEHAMPTON FAVOURITES.

4. *Beach donkeys.* Described as 'Littlehampton Favourites', as indeed they were, these animals were a regular sight on the Green and sands at Littlehampton every summer. Although regarded as lowly and insignificant, they brought pleasure to hundreds of young children, working very hard in their own gentle and uncomplaining way. To some youngsters the donkeys on the beach were the very epitome of an ideal summer holiday by the sea and often particular individual animals became special favourites. Also in the picture can be seen a cart drawn by two goats. These were also seaside favourites with the children, although possibly not always quite so docile as the humble mokes.

5. *Beach animals*. A further picture of the popular donkeys and goats, assembled with some of their public and also their attendants – not much older than the paying customers. The period is about 1908 and the sender of the card has written: 'This is to remind you of Brighton, only it is Littlehampton.' This was obviously a reference to the donkeys and goat carts which were also to be found at Brighton at this time. From the late nineteenth century, Littlehampton had been considered an ideal holiday venue for families with young children. The firm, clean sands and the seemingly endless Common were ideal playgrounds, and the locals did their best to provide the kind of innocent pastimes which would be acceptable to both the children and their Edwardian parents.

6. *Goat cart on the Green.* This was 1914 and on the long stretch of grass between the road and the beach could be found these attractive little goat carts, ideal conveyances for tiny tots – too small for the backs of the donkeys on the beach. Adults may have found Littlehampton a trifle dull at times, but young children were forever enchanted by this huge expanse of cropped grass, completely lacking in any sort of 'Keep off' notices. When the attractions of playing ball or just running around palled, there were still the gentle sands a few seconds away.

7. *Punch and Judy*. This was Uncle Charlie and his ever popular Punch and Judy show on the beach in the late 1920s, complete with Dog Toby. Uncle Charlie, who obviously loved children (he just had to!), had a conventional outfit at this time, and my own memories are of a very entertaining show, only marred by the part of the performance when the 'bag' came round. At this point, I discretely faded away, for as much as I loved Uncle Charlie and Punch, my finances were seldom capable of supporting them in a tangible way. Uncle Charlie always dressed very neatly in white trousers, blue Naval blazer and yachting cap, giving the impression of a retired mariner. His show was very much part of my childhood, as I am sure it was of many other youngsters'. One just couldn't envisage Littlehampton without Uncle Charlie and his Punch and Judy.

Uncle Tony

Uncle Charlie

8. *Punch and Judy*. Uncle Charlie, a little more portly perhaps and with the addition of Uncle Tony, in the 1930s. By this time the straight puppet show had been added to and moved on to the Green. It was now known as 'Children's Corner' and included conjuring, ventriloquism (two dolls who talked to each other), as well as the old favourite, Punch. There were two shows each day and the financial contribution had been upped to twopence. Once more I took part in the earlier part of the proceedings, finding urgent business elsewhere when the clink of coins was heard. Poor Uncle Charlie – I hope there were not too many children as impecunious as myself in his audiences.

BANDSTAND, LITTLEHAMPTON.

9. *Bandstand and band enclosure.* A group of well-used buildings at the sea end of Banjo Road (laid out in 1905) in the centre of the Green in the 1920s. There was room for 500 dancers or 1,500 listeners, with a café and a sunken garden. The programme for the 1926 summer season included the bands of the 2nd East Yorkshire Regiment, the 1st South Wales Borderers, the 1st Northern Fusileers, the Royal Artillery – Portsmouth, and the Royal Army Ordnance Corps. By the 1930s some of the evening entertainments went on until midnight.

THE PAVILION ON THE GREEN, LITTLEHAMPTON.

25

10. *Pavilion on the Green.* A rather barrack-like building as it was in the 1920s and '30s. It was sited at the western end of the Green, close to the Coastguard Station, and seated 500. Typical seaside concert parties performed here, with a change of programme weekly. In addition entertainers such as the Russian Ballet and well-known orchestras and children's shows were also booked. In 1926 the visiting artists included Murial George and Ernest Butcher, The Roosters Concert Party, the Piccadilly Follies, and Leslie Weston's Entertainers – names which may strike a nostalgic note with anyone who spent their summer holidays at Littlehampton at around that time.

11. *Picnic on the Green.* This is the early 1920s and the Stenning family from Broadwater, near Worthing, are enjoying one of their regular picnics at Littlehampton, complete with their own teapot. The father, Leonard Stenning, had a postman friend, Mr. Chandler, who owned an old taxi, which seated six plus children, plus driver. This picture shows off the current fashion in ladies' headware rather well. Those who were not equipped to make their own tea, could obtain trays from the old lifeboat house, which by this time was functioning as a café. Also in the background can be seen the old coastguard cottages, built between 1843 and 1850 to house the men who were not allowed to work in their own home area, where they would have had too many friends in the local community.

12. *John Bull?* The first of a couple of mystery photographs (perhaps a reader can assist). This appears to be the Green, with the buildings of South Terrace in the background. Judging by the clothes it would seem to be the 1920s. The identity of the horserider is not known, although he seems to be in a John Bull or Pickwickian type of costume. Most people who have seen this picture, guess that he may have been taking part in a local carnival. Littlehampton was always fond of its parades, whether for Carnival Day, a circus visit, or Bonfire Night. Whoever he was, he was obviously very pleased with life.

13. *Bungalow tea rooms, c1923*. Like most towns at this time, Littlehampton had a plethora of tea rooms and cafés. With few restrictions or rules to be observed, it was an easy thing to open one of these charming little establishments, some merely a front room in a private house. The Bungalow Café in Beach Road was one of the town's best and most popular meeting places for 'Dainty teas and Suppers' as their advertisement had it. The same advert also promised dancing every Tuesday from 8 to 11 for the modest charge of one and sixpence (7$\frac{1}{2}$p).

THE LAKE, LITTLEHAMPTON.

01389

14. *The Oyster Pond, c1910.* This was a small lake, man-made in the 18th century to store the oysters after they had been brought ashore by local fishermen from the oyster beds. When these languished in the late 19th century, it was turned into an ornamental lake for model boats. Although it then bore the official title of 'The Lake', most people still called it 'The Oyster Pond'. This attractive picture shows not only some of the children who used the lake, but as a backdrop the Arun Mill and the coastguard cottages. But not only youngsters used the pool – adults too brought extremely ornate and expensive model boats to sail therein. My own memory is of sailing a very cheap sailing boat, which persisted in capsizing in spite of all my efforts to keep it upright. Its condition was not improved by having stones thrown at it, to entice it back to the edge. At the same time, I was assailed with pangs of jealousy when I observed the beautiful model yachts which were tenderly lowered into the lake by their affluent owners.

15. *Regatta on Oyster Pond*. As well as the everyday joys of the model boating lake, there were weekly competitions for the more serious model boat owners, organised by the local model yacht club. In addition the Littlehampton watermen organised annual regattas on the river and children's regattas on the lake. In aid of the local hospital, these events were full of slap-stick comedy from the men who were so much at home on the water they could afford to take a few liberties with it. There was the ever-popular comic policeman, and always the town band, the latter taking part in a competition to row across the lake with one musician playing whilst the other did the rowing and steering. This picture is from a card posted in 1912, and the sender has written on the reverse: 'Grace and Iris had a lovely seaweed bath this morning.'

16. *H.M.S. Shirley.* My second mystery picture, but one which I feel sure someone will recognise. It shows a miniature boat, apparently an interwar battleship or cruiser, on the Oyster Pond, although the caption on the card implies that the photograph had been taken in Butlin's Amusement Park. This was built very close to the lake in the early 1930s, and included an artificial stretch of water with 'water dodgems', but this is certainly not the water shown in this picture. In the left background can be seen part of the big 'Thriller' amusement, which was part of Butlin's Park. The postcard is by J. White and Son, very well-known local photographers (1874-1968), but all who have seen the card confess themselves puzzled by the boat or the occasion.

Littlehampton (south).

17. *The Green.* Nearly a mile long, Littlehampton's famous Common, or 'The Green' as it was usually known, was an essential part of the particular allure of 'The Children's Paradise'. In the 1830s farmer Oliver's sheep grazed on the lush grass and there were plenty of mushrooms to be gathered at the appropriate times and seasons. Horse riding was popular, and well-organised horse races were held up to the 1860s. When these were taking place, the Green was covered with booths, tents and temporary eating houses. Later in the 1920s and '30s 'Keep Fit' classes were held here in the mornings during the summer and a group of young lady dancers, sponsored by a national daily newspaper, performed regularly. More recently the Green has had its own very popular miniature railway. This picture is on a card posted in the 1920s by a holidaymaker who had just arrived and commented that the weather was very warm and the sea very wet.

22 *LITTLEHAMPTON. — South Terrace. — LL*

18. *South Terrace.* A picture from the early part of this century of the houses built in varying styles between 1803 and 1820, overlooking the Green. In the scene are a fine collection of horse-drawn vehicles typical of the period, although why they are lined up so conveniently for the photographer is not clear. As often happened on holidaymakers' postcards, the position of the sender's holiday apartment has been marked, and the question is posed on the message side: 'Is it not a fine position?' It certainly was, with the view across the open common to the beach and the sea. No doubt the person who received the card was suitably impressed.

Empress Maud Road, Littlehampton

19. *Empress Maud Road.* This card dates from about 1904, although the buildings are from the period 1888-1898. This was part of South Terrace running from Granville Terrace to Pier Road, although the separate name went out of use in the 1920s. Empress Maud, who was Queen Matilda (widow of a German emperor), landed at Littlehampton on her way to claim the throne of England in 1139.

19 *LITTLEHAMPTON — Beach Hotel.* LL.

20. *Beach Hotel.* Always Littlehampton's best-known hotel, this picture shows it around 1909. Its origins were in c1775 when the Beach Coffee House was built. This was followed in 1887 by a hotel adjoining the original buildings. When the Coffee House was constructed, it would have been very near to the old Littlehampton windmill, which dated from about 1740 and was removed c1825. For several years the hotel advertised itself as 'The prettiest and most uniquely situated hotel on the south coast... within a 100 yards of the sea'. The sender of this card was not content with completely filling all the available space on the address side, but continued around the picture also.

21. *Fountain on the Green.* A view of the old drinking fountain c1905. It was erected, not as many such monuments to commemorate Queen Victoria's Diamond Jubilee, but just slightly later to mark the coronation of King Edward VII. It is still remembered with affection by many older residents and, as I recall it, was not only useful on a hot summer's day, but was also quite an attractive piece of Edwardiana. For reasons unknown, it was removed during the Second World War. The picture has the feel of Edwardian England, with the spotless clothes of the adults and children and the comfortable stability of the Beach Hotel as a background.

LITTLEHAMPTON. The Hillyers.

22. *The Hillyers*. A grand Regency house, part of South Terrace, c1903. Once run as a boys' school by the Reverend W. Philpott, it then became the Princess Louise Children's Hospital, and after that the Mary MacArthur Holiday Home for Working Women. In 1930 it advertised itself as a 'Homely Christian boarding house with temperance principles'. Those who were lucky enough to stay there must have fully appreciated the wonderful position with its fine open view to the sea.

Pier & Harbour.
Littlehampton.

23. *Pier and lighthouse.* A photograph from c1908. It shows most of the diminutive pier or jetty, with one of its graceful lighthouses completely in scale. There is also a bonus with the sight of the much-loved tug boat 'Jumna' bringing out a sailing ship. The pier was formed when the old east jetty was improved in 1873. It was always very much part of my childhood, and one of my earliest memories concerns a small group of slot machines on the beach side of the pier, in which I was never allowed to even consider inserting one of my precious pennies on a Sunday. Other personal memories of the pier include the time when as a child I sat at the extreme point and pretended that I was in charge of a real boat, with the sea on either side. Another occasion which I recall with great pleasure was when a friend and I with a hook and line (but no rod) used pieces of our sandwiches as bait and caught an unusual and quite large fish from the river side of the pier – much to the astonishment and envy of the serious fishermen!

24. *Lighthouses*. This was the lighthouse at the entrance to the tiny pier c1909. It was one of two, complementing each other, which were affectionately known as 'pepper and salt'. Unfortunately they were demolished in the Second World War and replaced by a far less attractive structure made of concrete. One further memory of the beach close to the pier, was of a wonderful day when a seaplane landed on the sea. Littlehampton was always a magical place to me as a child, but this was something of which dreams are made – at least so it seemed to one small boy.

Lighthouse & Pier
Littlehampton

LITTLEHAMPTON MILL

25. *Arun Mill.* A c1912 picture of the old tower windmill that stood for many years close to the harbour mouth. It was built in 1831-1832 by Henry Martin of Bognor, being operated during its life by several different millers, but ceasing active life in 1913. It was sadly demolished early in the 1930s by Billy Butlin, who had purchased the site of which it was a part, to build a grand amusement park. In fact the mill survived the opening of the amusements for a short time, but eventually had to go. It was said that Mr. Butlin regretted his decision to have it removed, as well he might. My grandfather, who had worked as a miller, took part in the demolition, managing to retain an old beam from the inside of the mill, which he used for many years as a clothes post in his garden. On it was inscribed the date 31st July 1868 – probably noting an early renovation of the mill.

SHERRELL
— AND CO.,

MILLERS,

Corn, Flour, Hay, Straw & Seed

MERCHANTS,

Arun Mill,

LITTLEHAMPTON.

Telegraphic Address:
' Sherrell, Littlehampton."

Cheques Crossed " London and County Bank, Littlehampton."

26. *Arun Mill.* Around 1900 the miller was Percy Sherrell and this is how he advertised his wares, with a picture of the mill and a horse and cart. The stone-ground flour was also made into bread and sold in a little shop in the town. Some customers preferred to buy flour direct from the mill and make their own bread, buying a pennyworth of yeast from the brewery in the High Street. This windmill, which is still remembered by many older folk with affection, was always known as Arun Mill or the Town Mill. There was in fact an earlier town mill which stood 100 yards nearer the sea. It is shown on a map of c1800, but was in ruins by 1820.

Littlehampton.

27. *The Worthing Belle.* A postcard c1910 shows the paddle steamer 'The Worthing Belle' leaving the harbour mouth. Built in 1885 as 'Diana Vernon' it was purchased by the Brighton, Worthing and South Coast Steamboat Company in 1901. After running regularly along the south coast until 1913, it was sold to a Turkish company and renamed 'The Touzia', being finally broken up in 1936. Earlier there were short-lived cross-channel steamships operating from Littlehampton. In 1863 the London, Brighton and South Coast Railway Company began services to the continent, and in 1864 another company began a similar service with chartered ships. But by about 1879 these were running at a loss and the venture soon came to an end.

LITTLEHAMPTON. The Harbour.

28. *The harbour, c1906.* This is a quiet corner of what must have been a fairly busy harbour around the turn of the century. Apart from the important business of shipbuilding, there were imports of such things as timber and coal, although the latter ceased in the 1950s. Of course there were other things as well; for instance around Christmas 1880 it was reported that 1,718 crates of mistletoe had been brought into the harbour for sale in the town. A lot of young ladies must have been kissed that Christmas! Nowadays it is the less romantic things such as aggregates that make up Littlehampton's import trade. Unusually the message on this holidaymaker's postcard is critical of the town, with the terse phrase: 'Was at Littlehampton yesterday, but did not think much of it.'

~ OUTWARD BOUND - LITTLEHAMPTON ~

29. *Sailing ship and pier.* A fine picture, but unfortunately this postcard is undated. It would appear to be from the 1920s or even '30s, when the sight of a ship of this kind would have attracted a small crowd to the pier The photo is by a local photographer, Mr. J. White, who had studios in the town. When coal was a major import, Littlehampton farmworkers sometimes augmented the crews of local colliers, plying between Littlehampton and Newcastle. A song from those days had the lines: *When our coal is all on board for 'hampton town we steer,/ And nothing else is in our heads, but old George Oliver's beer,/ We face all stormy weather and we batter through every gale,/ When the outer light is out of sight, its then we set our sail.* Apparently George Oliver was the landlord of the Rose and Crown pub. The song was noted from a retired coasting seaman in 1911, and again from another old singer in the 1930s.

30. *Pleasure boat*. This photograph has been carefully annotated on the reverse side: 'Taken June 27th 1915. Nellie's 21st Birthday. Motor trip up the river to Black Rabbit.' If only all owners of photos were so precise! This is a typical motor boat used for transporting holidaymakers up the Arun at this period. The accent is on safety, rather than looks or speed. One of those on board is an English 'Tommy', not surprising in view of the date of the card. The Black Rabbit mentioned, is a very popular restaurant on the river at Arundel, which for a long time has been a popular stopping place for boats from Littlehampton. When my parents planned their summer holiday at Littlehampton staying with my grandparents, a boat trip to the Black Rabbit was always a 'must'.

31. *Pleasure boat.* This picture is of a girls' club outing c1914. (The owner of the card has apparently identified herself with a cross.) The girls' club was in Kentish Town, London, and was run by a very overworked clergyman, the Reverend George Smisson. Each year they had a week's holiday in Littlehampton, around forty girls plus some children and helpers, staying at the Green Lady Hostel for Working Girls in East Street. The green fields and sunny beaches of Sussex must have made a welcome change from their normal surroundings.

32. *Pleasure boats.* I couldn't resist one further river trip photograph, this time from the 1920s. What makes this one a little special is the inclusion of what appears to be a band in the second boat (presumably Britannia I). I do not know anything about the occasion, although they must have had a lot of fun with their musical accompaniment. But how unfair to those on Britannia II, who appear to be without any musicians. But perhaps they preferred it that way!

33. *S.S. Dagfrid*. Aground in the river, 25th October 1924. It appears to be carrying a cargo of timber. Littlehampton has been a harbour since very early times, but over the years there have been constant problems at the harbour mouth due to shifting shingle. Two piers were built in 1735 to impede the flow of the shingle and in 1825 £20,000 was authorised to deepen the harbour. During the First World War the military attempted to improve matters with high explosive charges, but without any permanent success. In the background can be seen the Golf Club House on the West Bank. The club was formed in 1889, and the Club House erected in 1894. It was burnt down in 1985. The golf course was in a fairly isolated spot, but this was probably welcomed by the members. Originally the only access from the town side was by a row-boat ferry.

34. *Continental coaster.* Another ship aground c1930. A similar picture to the last, showing the Golf Club House on the West Bank. A fort was built on that side of the river in 1854, although it was little used and was largely dismantled by 1891. Apart from this there was little excitement on the West Bank, apart from the occasional visits to the golf club of celebrities such as the future King George VI, then Duke of York, and Sir Harry Lauder, the renowned Scottish comedian. They all had to make use of the little rowing boat which served as a ferry between the two banks of the river for many years.

35. *'Brothers Freeman' lifeboat.* The launch in 1904 of the last conventional lifeboat to be used at Littlehampton. As can be seen this was an oared boat and it remained in use until the 1920s, when powered boats came into use. Littlehampton then had no lifeboat of its own for forty years, until in 1976 it received the first of the new inshore inflatable rescue boats, which had been bought with money collected by viewers of the Blue Peter children's television programme. 'The Brothers Freeman' had a new house close to the river, with a concrete slipway, replacing an older house nearer to the sea front. (Both have since been used as cafés.) The boat was paraded round the town, together with the town band. Similar parades were then held each year on an annual 'Lifeboat Day'.

36. *Mystery ship*. This was described to me as a 'mystery ship', although it is not really a mystery, as it was the 'Argo' with dazzle camouflage, moored at Littlehampton's Railway Quay for dismantling after the First World War. During the war the harbour was very busy, and at the end much German material was brought in, and this was one of several such vessels which ended their lives here. The lady who lent me this photograph said her father had worked on the dismantling of the 'Argo'.

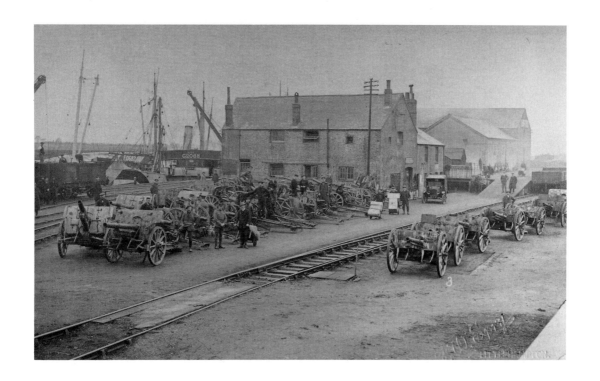

37. *Railway wharf.* Captured German guns at Littlehampton in 1918. During the war the government took over the railways and much of the port facilities, the bulk of munitions and war stores for France being sent from Littlehampton and Newhaven. 2,098 transports were loaded at the former port for France and overseas. Things were a little different in the Second World War. At Littlehampton priority was given to building harbour launches, shallow-boat troop carriers and landing craft. Many Littlehampton boats went to Dunkirk and upon their return, were fitted with special plaques.

38. *High tides.* Flooding at Fishermans Quay, 16th December 1910. Like most coastal towns, Littlehampton was often afflicted with flooded streets, particularly those near to the river. Several picture postcards exist showing such flooding, including one of the bus station in East Street. But most of the time things were very different. Littlehampton has always had a very good record as far as sunny days are concerned. In 1921 it could boast of over 1,945 hours of sunshine, and over a period of five years in the 1920s, the average number of sunshine hours was 1,852 yearly. As the Guide Books of this period said: 'A perfect climate for children, invalids and the aged.'

14 *LITTLEHAMPTON. — The Floating Bridge and Ferry. — LL.*

39. *Floating bridge, c1900.* The original manner of communicating with the West Bank was by a ferry row boat, as shown on the right of this photograph. The very idea of a conventional bridge met with much opposition, but in 1824 an act was passed for an alternative, a chain ferry. A year later this was built by Thomas Isemonger, the Littlehampton shipbuilder with a yard in River Road. The original wooden vessel was replaced in 1870 by an iron pontoon. Thomas Walker Horsfield in his monumental 'History and Antiquities of the County of Sussex', published in 1835, gave the floating bridge his approval stating: 'There is nothing to alarm the most spirited horse or the most timid lady.' In fact, the rather awkward-looking contrivance was often a wee bit temperamental, although it survived in service for around eighty years.

40. *Floating bridge.* A picture which shows the details of this unusual piece of maritime engineering. This picture was taken in about 1904, when the floating bridge was accidentally stranded. The building on the left was Harvey's joinery shop and next to it Mr. Hilder Harvey's house. Harvey's were well known locally as shipbuilders, being responsible for many fine vessels. The firm finally went out of business c1921.

41. *Floating bridge*. A sad picture as the old floating chain bridge which had been in use for around eighty years, is taken out by a tugboat for its first glimpse of the open sea. This was in 1908, when it was towed away to Southampton, sold, it was said, for a mere £40, ending its days converted into a houseboat. But I doubt whether many people spared a thought for an old friend, as most had their attention taken by the new swing bridge – as the next picture shows.

42. *Opening of swing bridge*. In August 1907 the foundation stone was laid for something which Littlehampton had been waiting for, or in some cases fighting against: a new road bridge across the Arun. This is part of the very big crowd on the opening day, 27th May 1908. The ceremony was performed by the Duke of Norfolk in full dress uniform of the Lord Lieutenant of Sussex. There was a public holiday, bands, flags, fireworks, illuminated boats on the river, fairy lights on the bridge, and a meal for 2,000 children on Rope walk. But all this only after a battle for and against the bridge had been fought, culminating in a referendum with a result showing 675 in favour and 213 against. The full story of the bridge is comprehensively told in Jack Thompson's book 'The Swing Bridge Story' (1979). In 1981 a new road bridge to the north was opened and Littlehampton's wonderful old swing bridge was replaced by a very utilitarian footbridge.

LITTLEHAMPTON BRIDGE

43. *The swing bridge.* The bridge which caused so much discussion before it was built, but which was accepted quite happily by Littlehampton folk once it had become a fact of life. The Reverend Henry Green, Vicar of Clymping, with George Groom, a grocer, and Neville Perrin Edwards, were the trio who had provided the driving force behind the proposal to build the bridge. The Reverend Henry wrote a song about the bridge, which was sung by Clymping schoolchildren, and also a book 'The story of the Littlehampton Bridge'. He was obviously a very happy man when he saw the open carriage carrying the Duke of Norfolk finally arrive – after some delay – to declare the bridge well and truly open. Although the bridge is no more, Amberley Chalk Pits Museum has a display of plans and photos of the bridge in its heyday.

LITTLEHAMPTON BRIDGE

TABLE OF TOLLS

(REVISED AS FROM 1st OCTOBER, 1923).

FOR EVERY:—

	s.	d.
Coach, Chariot, Chaise, Hearse, or other such like Carriage with four wheels, with horse, including return journey on same day	1	0
For each additional Horse		6
Chaise, Chair, or other such like Carriage with two or three wheels, with horse, including return journey on same day		6
For each additional Horse		6
Waggon, Wain or Dray, or other such like Carriage with four wheels, with horse, including return journey on same day		9
For each additional Horse		6
Cart, Dray, or other such like Carriage with two or three wheels, with horse, including return journey on same day		6
For each additional Horse		6
Horse, Mule or Ass, laden or unladen and not drawing		3
And the same returning.		
Weekly Ticket for Horse and Vehicle . 9s.		
Score of Oxen, Cows or Neat Cattle, and so in proportion for any less number	1	8
Score of Calves, Hogs, Sheep, Lambs, or Dogs, and so in proportion for any less number		10
Foot Passenger		1½
Weekly Ticket for Foot Passenger . 6d.		
Hundred-weight of Goods. Wares, Merchandise, Matter, or Things not being in any Carriage drawn by any Horse or other Beast, or drawn or propelled by mechanical power, or upon any Horse or other Beast		6
And so in proportion for any less weight.		
Car, Van and Lorry, drawn or propelled by mechanical power, including the return journey on the same day:		
Under three tons in weight		9
Weekly Ticket for Car, Van and Lorry . 10s.		
Over three tons and under five tons in weight	2	0
For every ton or part of a ton over five tons in weight		6
Trailer to a Car, Van and Lorry drawn or propelled by mechanical power, including the return journey on the same day:		
Under three tons in weight	1	0
Over three tons and under five tons in weight	2	0
For every ton or part of a ton over five tons in weight		6
Motor Bicycle or Tricycle, with Driver, (each way)		3
" " " " including Sidecar		4
Weekly Ticket for Motor Cycle, with or without Sidecar . 2s. 6d.		
For every other **Bicycle and Tricycle** (each way)		1½
WEEKLY TICKET FOR BICYCLE . 1s. without sidecar.		
Trailer to a Bicycle or Tricycle, including the return journey on the same day		3
Passenger on a Vehicle drawn or propelled by mechanical power, plying for hire at separate fares (other than the driver and conductor)		1½
Infant Carriage (including occupant and one attendant), (each way)		1½
Goat Chaise " " " and return journey		6

No Vehicle shall carry at one time on the Bridge (including the weight of such vehicle) more than twelve tons. Penalty £5, in addition to compensation for injury or damage.

Town Offices,
Littlehampton.

ARTHUR SHELLEY,
Clerk.

W. ——, Printer and Stationer, 19 Surrey Street, Littlehampton.

44. *Swing bridge toll board.* The bridge was a very useful source of revenue to the Littlehampton Council for many years. Here is the board which served to remind the public how much it would cost them to cross the bridge. A local legend has it that the Duke of Norfolk said that if his new baby arrived before or on the opening day, and if it was a boy, then the bridge would be free. The baby was a boy, but was four days late arriving, so tolls were charged. What a lovely story, even if rather unbelievable! The old toll booth and its board may now be seen at the Amberley Chalk Pits Museum, which is situated some way up the river from Littlehampton, but may be reached by boat from there.

45. *Smuggler's boat.* 'The Lapstone', an old clinker-built houseboat, with a most unlikely-looking thatched roof. Nicknamed the 'Noah's Ark' by the locals, it was permanently positioned on the river next to the 'Arun View' inn. Local legend has it that it has been used as a home by a smuggler around 1830. It was removed c1908 (when the new bridge was built) and Littlehampton lost a unique curiosity. Undoubtedly there was smuggling carried on in the river area of the town, as there was all around the coast of Sussex. It has been said with some truth that smuggling, with fishing and agriculture, was one of the three main industries of Sussex for many years.

46. *Thatched shops.* A much more common use for thatch was as roofing for houses, but perhaps less often shops. These two thatched shops once stood in the High Street, as can be seen in this picture dating from the 1880s. One shop was Nutters, the greengrocers, and the other Tommy Banfield's poultry and game business. In 1889 they were both pulled down to make way for Clifton Road. What a wonderful tourist attraction they would be today, if they had been allowed to remain.

47. *High Street, c1906.* A lively scene from the beginning of this century, with the pedestrians making as much use of the roadway as the few wheeled vehicles. The sign of the Crown Hotel can be seen on the left, also Mann's 'Cash Drapery Stores'. On the right was Charles Sparks and Son, who advertised themselves as 'Auctioneers, Valuers, House and Estate Agents, Cabinet Makers and Upholsterers'. Earlier still, in the 19th century, the High Street must have been an even more exciting place, for old accounts speak of a huge elm tree, opposite the Dolphin Hotel, which held joints of meat hanging from its branches, belonging to a butcher who had his shop nearby. On Fair Day (26th May) an old woman was to be found under this tree, selling trinkets. The tree was cut down in 1820.

Littlehampton.   High Street.

48. *High Street.* Another view of Littlehampton's main street, this time c1900, showing Smart's Corner. This was the oldest part of the street and was a popular place to meet one's friends, as I am sure it still is. Smart started in business in 1836 as a chemist, wine merchant, newsagent, tobacconist and vet. His adverts spoke of such articles as lemonade, soda, potash and raspberry vinegar. (It is not only in the present century that businesses have increased their turnover by stocking several different kinds of merchandise.) On the right is the Cyrus Temperance Hotel and a gentleman appears to be driving a donkey across the road. (One of the beach donkeys, perhaps.) As usual at this period there is little wheeled traffic and the pedestrians have time to stop and stare at the photographer.

49. *High Street.* A further view, this time c1907, showing rather more of the shops on the side opposite Smart's Corner. The traffic has increased somewhat and this time the animal population is represented by a lone dog. Well in this picture is Townsend's Bazaar, a wonderland of model yachts, kites, seaside toys and more prosaic things such as suitcases, china, glass and hardware. Later on the building of Littlehampton's Arcade enabled Townsend's to extend right round the corner and into this new shopping area. Townsend's, who probably sold copies of this postcard, cunningly painted in their own name much more clearly on the side of their building, so that it stands out far more than it would have done in an untouched photograph.

Church Street, Littlehampton

50. *Church Street.* A charming view, possibly from around 1890, although the postcard was sent in 1909. I am sure the photographer was thrilled to get this picture of not only a thatched cottage, but a group of sheep. However, the latter were not really all that unusual, even well into this century, as sheep were invariably driven along both country and town roads. The site is near the present junction of Goda Road, which was formed in 1907. The lovely cottage was a victim of road widening. (Countess Goda was sister of Edward the Confessor.)

51. *The Council Offices.* Again Church Road, but a view a good deal later than the previous picture. This was the early 1930s, when the Manor House, which had started life as a farmhouse, became the new Council Offices (moved from Beach Road). The builder's board is still visible and on the right are new public toilets and new entrance pillars to what is now the car park. All a little different to the old town pump, which a few years before had stood here. The photograph, taken by local photographer Mr. White, is from the High Street. The cars will probably evoke a feeling of nostalgia in many viewers, although the toilet block looks as if it could have been built yesterday. The Town Museum is now in this building, having been started in the Library, later functioning in River Road for many years.

52. *Norfolk Road.* A very nice c1900 view of one of the town's less often photographed roads, with a number of small shops and even more apartments. In the picture we can see the shops of Miss Annie Flatman (greengrocer), William Latter (butcher), Joshua Freeman Cobden (farmer and dairyman) and the sub-post office. Outside the dairy are two of the typical milk roundsman's handcarts of this period. I cannot resist adding this little story about Norfolk Road, from 1889: At the south end of the road a local band played regularly. One day a 'German band' started to play in the same spot and the local men obligingly set up further away. The visitors followed them, whilst the road's residents urged their own men not to give way. For nearly an hour both bands played against each other, with the town crier and his bell adding to the din. Around 300 people gathered and eventually the interlopers left; and the local men played a thumping 'God Save the Queen' and took up a good collection.

53. *Kings Arms*. Another view from the same period, of the Kings Arms public house in River Road. The lady outside the ivy-covered building is probably Mrs. Mary Ann Creese, the landlady, with her dogs. There were no less than six public houses in this busy road, which must have been a hive of activity at this time, with its wharfes, warehouses and workshops. Some of the local businessmen also lived in the road, near to their enterprises. No doubt the many men and masters who frequented the road, all had their own favourite drinking houses.

54. *Gloster Bakery*. A popular shop in the late 1920s, the Gloster Bakery in Gloucester Road, run by R.J. Pegrum and Son. There are two of the covered hand carts, beloved of bakers at this time, and an early delivery van. Miss Audrey Robinson, who contributed this postcard, remembers going to this shop regularly for her parents, to collect bread and cakes. She also remembers Mr. and Mrs. Thatcher, who are standing in the doorway. This was the time when bread and cakes would have been made on the premises, with wrapped and sliced bread still a thing of the future. Bakers were often asked by their customers to bake home-made cakes and puddings in their ovens.

55. *Clark and Robinson's shop.* This was in Terminus Road c1900, although their head office was in the High Street. The road was renamed when the railway station was built in 1863 – previously it had been known as Ferry Road. The wonderful collection of mangles, wringers and other items of garden and household machinery outside the shop, will bring back memories of the manner in which so many shops of this kind displayed their wares at this period. I often wondered where all the items were stored when the shop was closed, and had a mental picture of all this merchandise spilling out onto the pavement immediately the doors were opened in the morning. Certainly no space was wasted and goods were even hung from hooks in the ceiling. Pity the poor shop assistants who had to cope with it all!

56. *Olympia Hall.* The flags were out on 16th March 1910 for the opening in Church Street of the Olympia Hall by Mr. W. Beldam, a local solicitor with offices in the High Street. The hall was built by Linfield and Sons in 1910 as a skating rink, becoming the Empire Theatre around 1912 and the Palladium Cinema in 1920. An advertisement from the latter period promised: 'Continuous performances. 3 to 10.30. Change of programme Mondays and Thursdays. Popular prices. 1/3, 1/-, 9d and 6d. One cool spot in the Summer. Telephone number 44.' Hard to imagine a cinema show of two films, plus newsreel, for 2½p, but some cinemas were able to offer even lower prices!

"THE OLYMPIC HALL" LITTLEHAMPTON
OPENED BY W. BELDAM ESPRE MARCH 16TH 1910

57. *Olympia Hall interior*. This was the rather barrack-like interior of the Hall in Church Street, presumably in the period when it had become a theatre. The stage appears to be set for a play and little space has been wasted in the auditorium; in fact one wonders how the patrons managed to squeeze their way to their seats. The seats nearer the stage look a trifle less uncomfortable than the hard chairs at the back.

LITTLEHAMPTON CHURCH. AS IT APPEARED IN 1824 PREVIOUS TO BEING PULLED DOWN

58. *Parish church.* Of the many available pictures of the parish church at many periods, I have chosen a postcard showing an early print of the building as it was in 1824. It is believed that a church had been in existence on or near this site since Saxon times, and it bears the early dedication of St. Mary. In 1824-1826 it was rebuilt at a cost of £3,000 – a hundred pounds being contributed by the Duke of Norfolk, who was Littlehampton's biggest landowner. In 1876, when a chancel was added, the then vicar took out the east window, which had survived from the earlier church, and the stonework was left in a corner of the churchyard. Later another vicar gave the stones away, but subsequently they were handed back to the church, and the 14th century window, cleaned and reassembled, was successfully reunited with the church in the west wall of the tower. The church was again rebuilt in 1934 to cater for the congregation of that time. Over the years it has evoked rather mixed feelings in the minds of the architectural experts. Nikolaus Pevsner in his 'Buildings of England' calls the 1934 rebuild 'eerie disembodied Gothic', but admits that the result is 'far more of a church than most religious buildings of the 1930s'.

59. *St. Catherine's Roman Catholic church, Beach Road.* The church was designed by M.E. Hadfield and built in 1863 on land given by the Duke of Norfolk. The cost of £4,000 was borne by the Duchess, and it was one of a group of five churches built by her in Sussex in honour of the five wounds of Christ. It was enlarged in 1883 and again in 1904 to meet the increase in numbers of parishioners. This picture shows the church certainly after the enlargement of 1883 and perhaps just after the second enlargement of 1904. I am not sure why the children are sitting along the front of the wooden fence – perhaps just to be in the photograph.

War Memorial, Littlehampton.

60. *War Memorial.* The pleasing War Memorial in Beach Road, which was unveiled in September 1921 and dedicated to the 217 men who died in the Great War of 1914-1918. (The names of those who died in the Second World War were added later.) The ceremony was performed by General Lord Horne of Stirkoke. The cost was met by subscriptions raised by a War Memorial Committee. This photograph c1920s shows the relatively rural surroundings of the memorial at that period – long before the large Arun District Civic Centre built close-by in 1986, was even thought about.

61. *'Lady Mary' bus.* A picture from the early years of this century, showing Norris's motor bus and conductor. In spite of the charming name, it was not a very comfortable ride, I fear, but at least the passengers had the luxury of curtains to let down at the sides, if the weather proved too inclement. Like many other small local bus firms in Sussex, the company was taken over by the growing Southdown group.

62. *Motor coach*. A photograph of a 1930 Leyland Lioness motor coach, taken in East Street at the Southdown bus depot. It had a removable roof for sunny days and sported a very fine enamel radiator badge. Private cars were still a bit of a luxury for most families, and motor coach trips were extremely popular and well patronised. A Southdown Bus Company advertisement at this period promised 'Daily Motor Coach Excursions, and a Littlehampton to London service'. The cost of the latter was 7/6d (37½p) single, 8/- (40p) day return, or 12/6d (62½p) period return.

LITTLEHAMPTON. L.B.S.C.R.

63. *Littlehampton railway station*. Several pictures of the exterior of the station have been published, but here is one of the interior of this standard-pattern London, Brighton and South Coast railway station, around the turn of the century. Built in 1863, it was demolished in 1938 in readyness for a new station, which was not actually built until nearly fifty years later, due to the outbreak of the war in 1939. For all that time a temporary wooden station served this busy, little, south-coast resort, much to the surprise of many tourists, who arrived for their first visit to the town, expecting something a little less like the American West in frontier days. The picture shows what was obviously a very busy station, with almost every bit of the platform filled with such things as hampers, sack trucks, trolleys and luggage. There is one of the obligatory penny weighing machines and of course the station clock.

64. *Locomotive at Littlehampton station*. One of the popular Stroudley D-Class tank engines, most of them being built at Brighton from 1873 onwards. This is No. 24 'Bramblytye' which dated from 1875. Each engine at this time had its own driver, who kept to that one locomotive, as it was considered that maintenance was much better in this way – as no doubt it was. One of my most vivid childhood recollections is of waiting in the old Littlehampton station to be admitted to the platform, whilst one of these little tank engines huffed and puffed away on the other side of the barrier.

65. *'Our local express'.* A cartoon on a postcard from the early 1900s, proving that critical comments on the railway system are nothing new. The first railway to run near to Littlehampton was the Brighton and Chichester line, opened in 1846. On this line the station serving the town was in fact a long way to the north. At about the same time, there was a proposal for the construction of a new line from Arundel Junction (later renamed Ford Junction). The new line was opened in 1863 with a station, goods yard and sidings at Littlehampton. The old station on the coast line was then renamed Lyminster, but was soon closed. (Now there is a proposal for a new station in this area.)

"THE CAMP"
4TH (S.W.) LONDON BATTALION B.L.B. AT LITTLEHAMPTON 1910

66. *Boys' life brigade.* A 1910 picture of the 4th London Battalion of the Boys' Life Brigade in camp at Littlehampton. The London boys must have enjoyed the sands and sea and were no doubt welcomed by the Littlehampton Company of the B.L.B. The movement which was organised on military lines, but with strong Christian and temperance principles, included such activities as drill, gymnastics, first aid, band musicianship, flag signalling and the like. It was open to boys of 10 years upwards, on payment of a small weekly sum – but all members were obliged to attend Sunday School or Bible Class regularly and to be total abstainers. The highspot of the year was the summer camp.

67. *Sanger's circus parade*. One of Littlehampton's many popular parades through the High Street, early in this century. This famous circus visited the town more than once and never failed to provide a spectacle with its own parade through the busiest roads of the town. Most such photographs show the elephants, but on this occasion the photographer has decided to concentrate on the horses. Apart from the procession, the background offers several things of interest. On the right is the shop of Linfield Brothers, who were stationers, printers, booksellers, librarians and publishers of the 'Littlehampton News' (every wednesday) and a Littlehampton Guide Book. Note the price tags on the goods hanging in the doorway and also the lamps which were at this period always outside the shop windows rather than within, for safety reasons.

68. *Peace procession 1919.* This was a big event, with a very long route, and was well-covered by the local photographers. This is a view of the parade in South Terrace, opposite the Beach Hotel. The pierrot in the photograph is Mr. J.R. Robinson, of the prominent Robinson family, who started in the shipping business in Littlehampton back in the mid-19th century. The two brothers who started the firm were both master mariners; the dominant partner, Joseph Robinson, living until 1897, having served on the Local Board for many years. The Mr. Robinson in this photo was the father of Miss Audrey Robinson, who helped me to compile this collection.

69. *Opening of public library*. This was in 1906, being the first such library in West Sussex. It was financed by the Carnegie Foundation. The elderly man with the white beard near the door is Mr. W. Beldam, a prominent Littlehampton solicitor, who was active in local affairs at this time. He can also be seen on picture No. 56 opening the Olympia Hall in 1910. The movement to open free libraries throughout the country was in its infancy at this time, but it quickly grew and became a very important factor in the spread of adult literacy.

70. *Harry Joseph's concert party.* Harry Joseph was probably the best known of all the local Littlehampton entertainers in the early 1900s. He began his career in 1892, although this is a photograph of his group taking part in a comic football match c1920. H.J. is on the left wearing a 'boater'. His company performed in the Victoria Hall (formerly St. Saviour's Church) and on the Green. He later opened the Kursaal Theatre near the Arun Mill, which was later to become part of Butlin's Amusement park. A Harry Joseph advertisement promised: 'Good class singing, ballads, popular and humourous songs, duets, trios, quartettes, concerted numbers, sketches etc.'

71. *Audience at pierrot show.* Possibly one of Harry Joseph's performances. The photograph is from 1908 and was sent by a little girl called Alice to her Mum in Clapham, London. (She has marked the group she is in.) The Harry Joseph company was probably the oldest established pierrot troop in the country. In 1911 he entered his performers in the London Evening Times Contest for seaside concert parties, and out of over 60 they were voted the winners, going on to perform at the London Palladium.

MR FRED SPENCER.

72. *Fred Spencer.* A little less famous locally than Harry Joseph, but still a very popular Littlehampton entertainer. His style was said to be more in the Victorian Music Hall vein; one of his characters was known as 'Mrs. 'Arris'.

The Spencerites. Named after the leader, Fred Spencer, this was a group of seaside entertainers who enjoyed considerable popularity in the town in the early 1900s (This photo dates from c1915.) The costumes are typical of the pierrot-type shows particularly associated with seaside resorts. The better groups performed in theatres, but there were also others who had to be content with the open air type of stage surrounded by deck chairs within an enclosure of some kind. A charge was made for the chairs, although it was often possible to get some flavour of the proceedings from outside the enclosure – which is exactly what I had to be content with on most occasions, except when an aunt or uncle could be persuaded to produce the necessary few pence.

73. *Alf 'Badger' Bowley.* One of the many Littlehampton 'characters', who went back to the 19th century, although this photograph was taken in the 1920s. He was obviously part of the fishing community, although how he acquired the name 'Badger' I have been unable to ascertain. Not so very long ago the Littlehampton folk were known as 'Hampton Shakers', due to working so close to the dampness of the river. As well as boat building, fishing was a considerable industry, and a familiar sight for many years was the fishermen repairing their nets on Fisherman's Quay.

74. *Three old salts*. On the Fisherman's Quay, outside the old mortuary (where the men mended their nets), in the 1920s/'30s. Left to right they are 'Weeny' Moore, 'Flatty' Ansbridge and a third gentleman unknown. This was the period when almost all working men had a nickname bestowed on them by their fellows, usually descriptive in some way of their appearance or their capabilities. The photograph was taken by Edmund Robinson (1897-1985). From my own childhood I can remember a local 'character', who frequented the fishing area of the town. He would appear each day with an old pram, on which he carried a large wind-up gramophone with a huge horn. On this he would regale the passers-by with an ancient 78-record; as far as I can remember always the same one (or perhaps it just sounded like it). The object of the exercise was of course to persuade his audience to part with a few precious pennies.

75. *Mrs. Corney*. When starting to assemble this collection, I resolved to stick entirely to the town of Littlehampton, rather than to stray into the surrounding area. However, when this photograph turned up, I felt I had to break my rule, as it is so delightful. The lady in the long gown and bonnet is Mrs. Corney at the Toddington Tea Gardens, owned by her family in the 1920s. (Corney was a well-known Littlehampton name.) The Tea Gardens were a favourite spot to visit, in the little hamlet of Toddington, which was an easily three-quarter-of-a-mile walk across the fields. Advertisements stated: 'Teas provided in meadow, garden or orchard. Cut flowers, fruit and vegetables. Buses every ½ hour. Swings, see-saw, stoolball etc.' Audrey Robinson, who helped with this book, remembered with pleasure her visits to the Gardens as a child living in Littlehampton.